Steam Memories on Shed: 1950's – 1960's

No. 65: Manchester Engine

John Hooper

Copyright Book Law Publications 2013
ISBN 978-1-909625-06-8

INTRODUCTION

This album features the engine sheds located basically within the boundary of the City of Manchester. That is: 9A Longsight; 13A Trafford Park; 26A Newton Heath; and 39A Gorton, as those four establishments were initially coded in the first British Railways shed code scheme. Each shed was quite different from the others in both layout and locomotive types allocated so that an eclectic mix can be presented. One thing common to all the sheds was the external condition of their locomotives which, in the main, were quite filthy but apparently mechanically sound.

Longsight shed is of course still in business and seems to go from strength to strength. On the other hand, Trafford Park and Gorton are simply history now but images from the heady days of steam locomotion still exist so that both establishments can be brought back to life, at least on film. Newton Heath is nowadays operated by Northern Trains and has the title Train Maintenance Depot, looking after a third of NT's fleet. Its future is 'assured' but in the ever changing economic and political world it seems that nothing can be taken for granted by anyone, anymore.

Hopefully the presentation of locomotives at all four depots, and the locomotive works adjacent to Gorton shed, is both balanced and representative of the period under review. Many of the illustrations available to the compiler have been left out simply because there was no more room. However, another opportunity might arise to show some of the images which were sidelined from the initial selection.

John Hooper, June 2013.

Cover Picture: See page 9.

Title Page Picture: Gorton O4 No.63767 stables at the top end of the shed yard on Sunday 15th June 1958. Note the short-lived 9H shed plate which had been introduced during the previous February when Gorton became part of the London Midland Region. By April 9H was dropped in favour of 9G (Northwich's old code) but 9H remained fitted to many for some time after the change of shed coding. The building in the background was the main erecting shop of neighbour Beyer, Peacock. *C.J.B.Sanderson.*

Printed and bound by The Amadeus Press, Cleckheaton, West Yorkshire
First published in the United Kingdom by Book Law Publications, 382 Carlton Hill, Nottingham, NG4 1JA

LONGSIGHT

The full glory of the twelve road shed which existed at Longsight into BR times. The date of this illustration is 20th September 1953, a Sunday, early afternoon judging by the shadows. The shed here consisted of a section containing eight dead-end roads, on the left, with a four road section which continued through into the north yard. That latter section had a hipped roof although by this date much of the roof cladding had been removed, a process which was to continue during the decade until no roof existed over those four long roads. The eight road section, with its twin pitched roofs was no better off as much of the cladding materials had been removed from those too. Most of the dilapidation was by design but a good portion had been inflicted by years of smoke damage combined with adverse weather. The whole twelve road building dated from 1870 and originally had three hipped roofs but in the early 1930s the LMS, unusually, saw fit to re-roof eight of the roads with two high pitched roofs with corrugated gables as here. The normal method of re-roofing LMS engine sheds during that pre-war period entailed building a pitched section of roof over each stabling road (as at Newton Heath in 1935). Radical changes were taking place in the 1950s and as funds became available, Longsight's engine sheds were being upgraded to modern, well-lit, spacious workplaces fit for the next generation of motive power. The eight road dead-end section was virtually demolished in 1956 and a new east wall was erected between what had been Nos.8 and 9 roads (numbered from the west) followed by a steel and glass roof; six roads replaced the original eight to allow a greater freedom of movement for fitters. By 1957 that shed was operational repairing steam locomotives but it was also ready for the diesels when they eventually came to Longsight. On the extreme left is the 1907-built carriage shed which had replaced some earlier locomotive accommodation dating from the earliest days of Longsight's existence. The single line of railway connected the north and south yards and was used mainly by engines working their way through the coal, water and ash servicing, and then returning to the north shed via the south shed yard. *F.W.Hampson.*

3

Visible on the right of the previous illustration, Stanier Cl.3 tank No.40077 is stabled outside the shed's offices on that glorious Sunday in September 1953. Longsight had four of this class allocated at this time, none, it seems, were looking their best but neither was much of the 9A stud at that time. The 2-6-2T is stood on one of the four through roads which would be left open to the elements after the demolition of the eight road section at this end of the shed. The roof over the four through roads at the other, north end, alongside the rebuilt north shed, had already been dealt with by the LMS just prior to BR coming into being. On the right is a somewhat lightweight footbridge which spanned the roads leading from the ash and coaling plants, not to mention the coal sidings alongside. When electrification finally arrived at Longsight in 1960, this bridge was replaced by a substantial pre-cast concrete structure with parapets high enough to deter anyone reaching over and touching the overhead. Masked by the 2-6-2T was the bay window of the Foreman's office which was set into the end gable and had a commanding view of anyone venturing down the steps of the footbridge. It wasn't easy 'bunking' Longsight but we did it often by various means. Just inside the 'shed' one of 9A's remaining pair of Compounds, No.41168 (41159 was the other), stables beneath the skeleton of the roof. By the time the new south shed was operational, the pair of 4P 4-4-0s had transferred away to Crewe North ending a long association between Longsight and the early LMS passenger motive power. *F.W.Hampson.*

Ten years on and the four through roads are still in use although changes have been afoot in the interim. This scene is dominated by the east wall of the south shed which was built in 1957 and featured large windows along its whole length to complement the natural light coming through the roof glazing. The trio locomotives featured have arrived for repairs which their own sheds could not carry out, hence a trip to the parent shed – Longsight. Nearest is Heaton Mersey's 8F No.48190 with a Cl.5 behind that, and a 2-6-4T bringing up the rear. The 8F could have reached 9A by a couple of routes, neither of which were straightforward but nevertheless manageable, and a nice morning out for any crew involved in the trip. The first would take the 2-8-0 west from 9F to Chorlton, Throstle Nest Junction, onto the MSJ&A line to London Road (sorry Piccadilly) and then up to Longsight. The alternative would take the eastwards route through Tiviot Dale, Woodley, Hyde Junction, Guide Bridge, and Ardwick to reverse for Longsight. The road nearest the shed was dedicated to allowing access to the fuelling rack for diesel locomotives. The two roads nearer the aforementioned office were reserved for the breakdown train and a stand-by locomotive in steam. When they eventually came to Longsight, electric locomotives were kept away from this part of the depot. *A.Ives.*

Turning the camera around by about sixty degrees clockwise, and stepping back to take in the view, we find Ivatt Cl.2 No.41217 on stand-by duties outside the shed offices on 28th June 1959. Part of the breakdown train, which was on constant call-out, can be seen behind. Arriving at Longsight in September 1958 from Barrow, No.41217 brought sister No.41221 along too. What they actually got up to in their time at 9A is unknown but they both left in July 1960 for the exotic surroundings of Widnes. Not looking its best on this Sunday in 1959, our subject nevertheless managed to survive until the last day of 1966 and became the last member of the class working on the LMR. A handful of the class working on the Southern stuck at it until the end of steam on that Region in 1967. Useful engines but the work they were designed to do was disappearing before all of them were put into traffic. A number have survived into preservation. *C.Campbell.*

6

The unmistakable head-on profile of a Caprotti fitted '5'. Arriving new from Crewe in February 1948, No.44748 spent the whole of its life working from Longsight, one of the few locomotives to do so. In this 3rd November 1963 portrait, the 4-6-0 is stabled inside the north shed. Ready for its next turn of duty, whatever that may be because the options for steam locomotives, no matter how efficient, useful, or young, were slowly being eroded by the growing band of diesels and electrics working the services formerly entrusted to these engines. Less than another year of operations remained for No.44748 before withdrawal in August 1964. We are standing at the rear, southern end, of the north, or back shed as it was also known, looking at the results of the re-roofing carried out on this building, also in 1948. Pre-fabricated concrete components were used throughout, BR adopting the techniques used by the LMS in their last spate of shed rebuilding prior to Nationalisation. Even though much of the roof cladding was patent glazing, daylight found it hard to penetrate windows which had not been cleaned since the day they were installed. *A.Ives.*

On the same day that No.44748 was inside the 'back' shed, 'Royal Scot' No.46140 THE KING'S ROYAL RIFLE CORPS was stabled outside on the westernmost road, alongside the carriage shed. Perusal of the floor to the left of the 7P will reveal the remains of a section of the wall from the original 1903 shed which was shortened by about a third of its length during the 1948 rebuilding; the inspection pits give some idea of the extent of the 1903 shed. Behind the 'Scot' is one of the LNWR coal stages which survived the 1930s modernisation at Longsight and was kept for emergency use in case of breakdown affecting the mechanical coal plant. At this time in 1963, No.46140 was a resident of 9A, its second such stint (the first one lasted from June 1954 to September 1959) having been transferred from Newton Heath during the previous June. Miraculously, considering the electrification and dieselisation of the main line services was all but complete, the 4-6-0 was kept at the Manchester depot for another year before managing to escape to Kingmoor where a further year's work beckoned before withdrawal in the final week of October 1965. *A.Ives.*

Going back in time to October 1961, Sunday morning of the first day to be precise, Crewe North 'Jubilee' No.45737 ATLAS looks like a vision of health as it simmers on the No.1 road of the back shed ready for its next duty. Admittedly the locomotive had received a Heavy General overhaul only seven months beforehand but nevertheless 200-odd days in service can generate a lot of dirt so it's obvious that Crewe had actually cleaned the 6P recently. This engine had never been allocated to Longsight, except for a seven week loan in 1949, so local enthusiasts would probably be enjoying seeing this 'Jubilee' on shed. Mention of its HG earlier was in fact its final heavy overhaul and visit to the works at Crewe. It was in works for an inordinate period of time – 12th December 1960 to 2nd March 1961 – compared with most but it was fitted with a speedometer at the time. At the end of March 1962 ATLAS left 5A and its cleaning gang for the last time and entered the realms of darkness at Newton Heath. It was to spend the rest of its life there until withdrawn at the end of May 1964. *I.S.Jones.*

Although the depot had a healthy allocation of the class, 'Royal Scots' had a fairly high turnover at Longsight, as was the normal practice at most of the Western Division sheds. At any one time during the 1950s, 9A could have a dozen or more of the class allocated. With the 'Jubilees' and the Patriots, straight boilered and rebuilt examples included, these 7P 4-6-0s worked the bulk of the London expresses. No.46106 GORDON HIGHLANDER, the 'odd-man-out' amongst the 'Scots' as it was the only one with straight sided, 'Britannia' type smoke deflectors, became a regular on the London workings from the summer of 1958 until the end of the summer timetable in 1960. Looking rather smart on 7th April 1959 outside the north, or back shed, it appears to be ready to work one of the Euston expresses with its driver lubricating what seems to be the buffer shank too. Note the brackets on the cab side, just above the number, which were fitted to carry the nameplate of the driver; such niceties were a short-lived experiment in BR public relations which was apparently not too popular with the enginemen – the niceties that is. *C.J.B.Sanderson.*

Longsight wasn't exactly brimming with conventional Stanier Class 5s but the later Caprotti version was quite a common sight at the shed virtually until closure to steam in 1965. This is resident No.44742 outside the north shed on the evening of 28th June 1959. Look past the filth enveloping the 4-6-0 and look instead at the massive steam pipes, the low running plate and the large cylinder box which contained that mass of complicated machinery and which made these locomotives work. They were quite different from the rest of the class but they made quite an impression on the authorities because although only nineteen of their kind were built during the transition period between the LMS and BR taking the reins, BR built a large number of the BR Standard version. Did they save money as regards the use of coal and water? Were they more expensive to maintain then the conventionally fitted engines? Did they cost more to produce – yes! Would they have saved BR lots of money eventually if steam was still the present motive power and if they had run their normal lifespan of 30–35 years? So, only one fact was certain, the others were either being answered or could never be answered. The engines were without doubt useful and Longsight often let them take charge of their London expresses, including the prestigious *MANCUNIAN*. No less than nine of the type were allocated to 9A at any one time in the 1950s, more than any other shed. *C.Campbell.*

Besides the eleven 'conventional' Caprotti's on Longsight's books, the shed was home to the two high-footplate versions, Nos.44686 and 44687, which were introduced as late as April and May 1951, and which incorporated lots of refinements not found in the Nos.44739 to 44754 batch. This is No.44686 on the north yard on that same Sunday evening in June 1959, backing away from the coaling plant. Both remained at Longsight until 1960 when the transitional changes of the forthcoming electrification, dieselisation, and the realisation that developments and refinement of steam motive power was at an end. No.44686 transferred to Llandudno Junction shed, where they had experience of the Caprotti valve gear, in April 1960 whilst No.44687 went to Crewe South in August. The latter shed of course had little if any knowledge of the workings of the Caprotti system and within a matter of weeks had sent their charge to Llandudno Junction too. In September 1963 another shed which was unfamiliar with Caprotti valve gear – Southport – had both of the hybrids thrust upon them. By hook and by crook the seaside shed managed to keep the pair operational until October 1965 and January 1966 respectively. *C.Campbell.*

A visitor from the Midlands, in the shape of a Bescot based Stanier 2-8-0, No.48762. Complete with a Fowler type, 3500 gallon tender (a hideous marriage if ever there was one), the 8F stables on the south shed yard on Sunday 24th April 1960. It was not until BR days that Longsight maintained a small fleet of 8Fs, the heavy goods work for much of the LMS period, and beforehand, being entrusted to a dozen or more G2 0-8-0s but by 1950 their numbers at 9A were down to just a couple, the Stanier eight-coupled taking their place. *J.Archer.*

At virtually the same spot on the south yard eight years earlier, in August 1952, resident Stanier 'Crab' No.42979 takes in the morning sunshine flanked by a 4F 0-6-0 and, behind, Crewe North Fowler 2-6-4T No.42308. At this time Longsight had just two of these useful and reliable engines which would be used for the likes of the overnight 'Camden Goods' turn. This mixed traffic 2-6-0 class was another which never came to 9A in any great numbers and during the period under review only three – 42960, 42978 and 42979 – were ever allocated for any appreciable time. Without doubt, Longsight's allocation was varied if nothing else, with seventeen classes from 0-6-0T to 4-6-0 7P gracing the yards when BR came into being. A decade later some fifteen different classes of steam locomotive were still on the books and added to the diesel types which had arrived by 1959, the variety remained. It is interesting to note that the BR Standard types, other than the 'Britannia' class, were never resident here in any numbers either; one or two did come and go but otherwise they made little impact on the ex-LMS standard classes. *K.H.Cockerill.*

A couple of locomotive views from 20th September 1953 illustrating two of the depot's loyalist types stabled at the east side of the north shed: Rebuilt Patriot No.45536 PRIVATE W.WOOD V.C. *(above)* was a long standing member of the 9A allocation, its name carrying a former Longsight railwayman's deed of Valour far and wide for all to see, and remember. Rebuilt in this form in November 1948, it was the penultimate class rebuild, and a regular on all the expresses originating from London Road. It ended its days at 9A and was withdrawn during week ending 29th December 1962. 'Crab' No.42889 was another long standing Longsight engine, at least during BR days. Wearing the badge of filth which afflicted so many locomotives in BR days, the 2-6-0 was a popular type amongst the 9A enginemen (universally so amongst ex-LMS sheds) and from small beginnings with only a handful in the early 1930s, the number rose to nineteen allocated at the end of the LMS. There was still a dozen attached to Longsight in 1960, No.42889 amongst them. *both F.W.Hampson.*

A familiar sight for local enthusiasts throughout 1960 and 61 was this small group of withdrawn locomotives dumped alongside the redundant wall of the former shed. The date is 24th April 1960 and the unlucky trio consisted 2P 4-4-0 No.40674, Stanier Cl.3 2-6-2T No.40084, and Stanier 1P 0-4-4T No.41907. The 2P still had a 'bag' on its chimney but this stemmed from storage during 1959 from which it was not resurrected and was instead condemned at the end of November 1959; the Cl.3 suffered similarly. As time went by this storage line started to attract more locomotives each month and in December 1961 the 4-4-0 and the 2-6-2T were sold to a scrap yard in Wigan and taken away. The 0-4-4T was taken to Gorton works and cut up there. The towering bulk of the coaling plant overlooks the scene as it had since 1934 when the aforementioned shed existed. *J.Archer.*

Joining the band of withdrawn engines at the north end of the shed yard in 1961 was Stanier Cl.4 No.42570. Its condition can only be described as deplorable which would be expected perhaps with any locomotive which had been withdrawn but the 2-6-4T had not been withdrawn when this photograph recorded its plight on Saturday 15th July 1961. The Cl.4 tank first came to Longsight's attention in June 1960 when it was transferred to Macclesfield (9C) after twelve years at Edge Hill shed. But when 9C was closed on 12th June 1961 No.42570 was re-allocated to Edgeley – on paper at least – but it probably never worked from 9B and was sent straight to Longsight for a check. It was promptly sent to the storage line and significantly was not fitted with a chimney cap. It was condemned in the first week of October and later sold to the same Wigan yard where the previous subjects had been sent, but not until the middle of 1962 did it leave Longsight. No.42570 was one of the first of its class to be withdrawn and when that event occurred, the Class 4 was only 25-years old. However, the 1960s was a period during which any steam locomotive, young or old, had to be in fine fettle if it was to escape an early meeting with the melting pot. *F.W.Hampson.*

Resident English Electric Type 4 D218 CARMANIA stables on the yard of the north shed on 3rd November 1963. This particular diesel-electric had been allocated to Longsight since 10th September 1960 on transfer from Edge Hill. The class was well established at 9A by this date, their growling exhausts discernible to those living and working adjacent to the main line from Manchester to Stockport. D218 is not looking its best in this illustration but that was a sign of the times when locomotive cleaning appears to have been fairly low in the order of priorities on BR. Not the first of its kind to be allocated to Longsight, this certainly was not to be the last either. The first to arrive was D217 on 8th August 1959 from Crewe North. It made quite an impression on everyone. Three weeks later two new examples arrived – D227 and D228 – and Longsight began a long association with an iconic class of diesel locomotive which was to last for more than twenty years. Alongside is one of the BR Sulzer Type 2s, another diesel class which became established at Longsight. *A.Ives.*

One of Longsight's shed outlets/inlets to the main line just north of Longsight station's Up platform. This scene was recorded on Sunday 28th June 1959 when Longsight was once again undergoing changes; a new two-road shed was being erected for the servicing of the forthcoming electric locomotives which would one day ply the routes to Crewe and Stoke and the main line to the south. The erstwhile passenger station had closed for normal traffic during the previous September but was still used for the occasional excursion train bringing day-trippers to nearby Belle Vue Gardens. However, the station was being brought back to life at weekends as a terminus for local services from Buxton, Crewe, Stoke and a host of others places round about this time whilst the re-signalling and rebuilding of London Road station was underway. Long distance services used Central, Exchange, Victoria and Mayfield. The gantry is pure LNWR but its life was coming to an end as colour light signalling was quickly replacing the old semaphores between Ardwick and Levenshulme; note the new building on the right which was part of that scheme. We shall return to Longsight in a future volume and take a look at the changes which took place after the end of steam and into the era of the electric railway. *C.Campbell.*

TRAFFORD PARK

Trafford Park in 1951 before alterations changed the front profile of the shed from the hipped roof style to the gable style. J10s are prominent in this view with No.65131 nearest and 65202 displaying its BR ownership as loudly as possible. *K.H.Cockerill.*

One of Trafford Park's 'mechanical' coaling plants; well sort of. This apparatus was located in the former LNER side of the shed building which was by now totally roofless and devoid of many of the stabling roads formerly therein. The whole shed premises at Trafford Park consisted of two mirror-image sheds and facilities joined together down the middle. The water tank above the rear wall for instance had a counterpart at its south end supplying water to the LMS engines. Such assets help prevent a lot of unnecessary paperwork, accounting and arguing. However, the GC and GN shared their half of the facilities whilst the Midland just got on with it in their own half. The GCR's locomotive fleet at this shed was somewhat greater than the dozen or so stabled by the GN so division of costs, etc., would have been sorted out accordingly. The BR set-up got rid of the need for partition and the shed became one big happy family sharing appliances like this for instance; a second similar conveyor was located just behind the photographer. The eagle-eyed amongst you will have spotted that the 'Black 5' being replenished on this Wednesday 22nd June 1966 was No.45150, a resident of 9E since November 1964, when it was transferred from Newton Heath. Contrary to its external condition, the '5' survived here until March 1968 when withdrawal took place. Note the painted notice on the door beneath the water tower, it reads '...Doors Clear...' yet somebody has left a sack trolley right outside! We love instructions don't we? *K.Gregory.*

A nice view from Sunday 25th July 1965 showing part of the rebuilt shed and illustrating the smaller pitch of the middle section of shed (just below the floodlights of a football stadium, the name of which escapes me) where everything once met. Except for the engines of course, note how clean and tidy the place appears to be under the clear summer sky. For the record Nos.45150, 43012, 44888 and 42066 were identified. No.45150 we have already met whereas No.43012 was a visitor from Heaton Mersey and which had started life in April 1948 at Bristol Barrow Road shed; it left 9F for North Blyth in August 1966 and was condemned there in April 1967. No.44888 was a new addition to Trafford Park's allocation and was ex Patricroft during the previous May. It went to Edgeley in March 1968 and managed to make its way to Lostock Hall via Bolton; it was amongst the last of BR steam in Black August 1968. No.42066 was another 'exotic' which had arrived from Aston that month. The Fairburn tank had started life on the Southern at Ramsgate; it moved on from 9E to Low Moor in May 1967 and was condemned shortly afterwards. *Trevor Ermel.*

Now then, here are a couple of pieces of ironwork with a difference! *(above)* Remember the nameplates which slotted into a bracket on the cab sides of locomotives which depicted the name of the driver? Well how about this 'Not To Be Moved' plate with the name of the fitter embossed! The date of the image is 24th September 1961. A nice innovation but were such practices in vogue at other sheds? *N.W.Skinner. (right)* This letter posting box, photographed circa 1952, was located at the shed but its exact position is unknown. However, it is of interest because it shows the owning company initials along with the initials of the two main 'shareholders'. But besides the obvious, what was its purpose? Internal mail!? Surely, nothing to do with the Royal Mail! What is interesting is that upon close inspection of the image, there does not appear to be any key holes, hinges, or breaks in the metal where a door or opening would be located. It must have been produced post-grouping because the three main partners of the Cheshire Lines – GCR, GNR and MR – could not have had plates evenly fitting on the cast panels as the post 1923 partners did. A curiosity certainly! Were any other examples known? Answers on a post card...! *K.H.Cockerill.* 23

One of Gorton's Fowler 2-6-4Ts No.42334 stables at Trafford Park in between working the Liverpool (Central)–Hull (Paragon) passenger services between Manchester (Central) and Guide Bridge – via the Fallowfield loop – where electric traction took over for the run over Woodhead to Sheffield. *Trevor Ermel.*

Mention earlier of the mirrored facilities at this former CLC shed is backed up by this illustration showing not just a bunch of filthy engines sheltering behind the redundant north wall of the shed, but also 'outside' of that is the coaling stage formerly used by the LNER. This image was recorded on Sunday morning, 20th September 1953 with the former LNER contingent still encamped in their section of the old shed, albeit roofless. An unidentified D10 'Director' hides behind the pair of N5s, with long term resident No.69364 prominent and No.69370 to its rear. *F.W.Hampson.*

Moving down the line of engines on 20th September 1953 we come across D10 'Director' No.62653 SIR EDWARD FRASER looking much like the other ex-GCR locomotives around this place! However, this 4-4-0 was just coming up to its fortieth birthday if an excuse was required. Having already transferred sheds fifteen times to get to Trafford Park for the second time in May 1950, it had one more transfer to perform before withdrawal when a move to Northwich in February 1954 would see it remaining as a regular over the Cheshire Lines system for a further eighteen months. Note the spring on the running plate; it looks like a visit to the sheerlegs is next. No.69370 on the left, departed from this shed on 27th April 1958 but instead of going to the scrapyard like most of its ilk, it transferred to Darnall for a couple of months but even that wasn't the end of it because Barnsley shed then wanted its services and kept hold of it for a further eighteen months – miraculous? No! Two General overhauls, complete with boiler changes took place after this photograph was recorded. Mexborough took it on in January 1960 and used it until it was eventually condemned on 10th September 1960, one of the last of its kind. *F.W.Hampson.*

On that same Sunday in September 1953, the ex-LMS side of the shed had a variety of locomotives on show, amongst them this Fairburn Cl.4 tank from Springs Branch, No.42121. WD No.90204 was another visitor but from nearby Belle Vue. To finish off the trio, the rather dirty Compound on the left was yet another weekend visitor, No.41151 from Brunswick, a shed which, like Trafford Park was a bit short on cleaners. Trafford Park may well have been one of the least attractive engine sheds on BR but the variety of locomotives it played host to made it one of the more interesting depots in the area. *F.W.Hampson.*

Probably the most iconic Great Central locomotive type ever built – the D11 'Director'. Extremely capable locomotives, they worked the cream of GCR express passenger services well into the Grouping period and were even pressed into service on the East Coast main line on Pullman services from Leeds. Only the coming of the Pacifics and LNER Standard classes pushed them onto secondary passenger services but nevertheless, they remained reliable and capable machines. The fact that the LNER expanded their number for service in Scotland shows the high regard that Gresley held for these engines. This is No.62662 PRINCE OF WALES at home on 14th June 1953, and looking rather splendid considering it hadn't been near main works in six months. It was the 4-4-0s first residency at Trafford Park – all of the class did a stint there during 1950 or 1951, some for longer than others – and nearly five years elapsed before it moved on to Northwich on 1st October 1955 but much of the time in Manchester was spent in store. It was this 'Director' which spent a week allocated to Newton Heath in May 1956 for reasons unknown. No.62662 ended up 'working' from Darnall shed from April 1958 but it was more a matter of storage for the Prince and the rest of the class because BR did not know what to do with them. Withdrawal took place on 8th August 1960 and the D11 was taken to Doncaster and cut up. *C.J.B.Sanderson.*

As mentioned previously, the bulk of the time spent at Trafford Park for most of the D11 'Directors' was in store. A filthy No.62664 PRINCESS MARY – what a contrast to 62662 – resides at the back of the shed on 14th June 1953, although not in store. Further detail of the water tower can be seen. *C.J.B.Sanderson.*

Another contrasting picture from June 1953 with a rather smart D10 'Director' No.62656 SIR CLEMENT ROYDS spruced up by the cleaning gang. All of the D10 class were renowned for the number of shed changes undertaken during their lifetimes; this engine managed twenty-one with the three years spent at Trafford Park being the penultimate transfer. Northwich was its final home. *C.J.B.Sanderson.*

Resident 'Jubilee' No.45628 SOMALILAND stables outside the former Midland side of the shed whilst rebuilding and re-cladding of the roof continues above on Sunday 14th June 1953. Trafford Park usually had half a dozen of these 6Ps for working the Manchester (Central)–London (St Pancras) expresses at this time. Even in World War Two they made up the bulk of the LMS allocation of sixteen locomotives with five or more in residence but this had risen to seven by Nationalisation, although not all of these had been here during wartime: Nos.5618, 5622, 5628, 5629, 5652, 5655, 5664. The 'Jubilees' had ousted the six resident Stanier Class 5s – Nos.5035, 5036, 5042, 5067, 5068, 5069 – which had been at Trafford Park from their introduction to the shed in 1935. No.45628 had been at Trafford Park since September 1939 and remained on the books until September 1956 when Longsight briefly required its services; it was back at 9E in November and stayed until July 1958 when it re-allocated to Kentish Town. It returned to Manchester briefly in the summer of 1961 to take on some of Newton Heath's holiday work; 'Britannia's' and diesels had taken over the Central–St Pancras expresses by then. *C.J.B.Sanderson.*

With shed roof repairs complete and everything back to normal, the locomotive population continued in steady decline at Trafford Park, as did, it appears, the cleaning of it charges. The date is Saturday 16th July 1955 and the Shed Foreman seems interested in 4P No.41114 (you will have to take my word for it) or its preparation. A fairly new member of the 9E Compound stud, this 4-4-0 had come from Llandudno Junction during the previous summer. This was another class which had a long association with the shed with four to six, depending on seasonal changes, being the usual number in residence. This illustration depicts a sunny afternoon with engine sheds doing what they did best – pollute the local atmosphere. Another 4P flanks a Millhouses Ivatt Cl.4 which is hiding between the 4-4-0s. *F.W.Hampson.*

Another 'Jubilee'!? Why not! Derby based No.45626 SEYCHELLES stables 'inside' the roofless shed in September 1951. Shedplate apart, you can somehow tell that this 6P was not a Trafford Park engine, but I can't quite put my finger on it. One of the shed's hallmarks is however visible in the shape of the piles of smokebox char left on the front platforms. Things got better, apparently. Trafford Park shed went through a number of shed district changes during the BR period. Starting out as 13A in 1948, in charge of its own district which encompassed Belle Vue, Heaton Mersey, Northwich, Brunswick, Walton-on-the-Hill, and Lower Ince, it became subordinate, in May 1950, to Longsight when the code 9E was issued and the 13 District was abolished, forever. A further change in January 1957 which seemed highly impractical on paper, took the shed into the Derby fold when it was given code 17F. That situation lasted just over a year and in April 1958 common sense prevailed and Trafford Park reverted back to 9E, the code it kept to closure. *K.H.Cockerill.*

Looking like a smoke free zone, the shed on Saturday 22ⁿᵈ August 1959 presented a cleaner image than depicted in earlier illustrations. Centre of attention is 3F 0-6-0 No.43400, a relative newcomer to 9E, which was simmering away and soaking up the early evening sunlight, the unfamiliar surroundings nothing like its previous home at Rowsley. Behind is resident 4F No.44392 which had transferred from Brunswick six years beforehand. To the left, stabled on the site of the roofless section of the old LNER shed was Fowler 2-6-2T No.40017 which was in store and about to be withdrawn. The new roof cladding has taken on the staining from numerous exhausts but it will last for the remaining years of the shed's lifetime and shelter many more locomotives before the shed closed in March 1968. One group of diesel locomotives which arrived at the shed in 1960 and 1961 was a batch of about a dozen of the Metro-Vick Co-Bos which had given so much trouble to the London Midland Region since their introduction in 1958 that the authorities decided to hand them back to the manufacturers for modification to their unreliable Crossley engines. Trafford Park was the storage point for the diesels prior to their being taken one by one to the former carriage works at Dukinfield where they were 'renovated'. By 1962 the whole class was back at work but had been sent to Cumbria. *N.W.Skinner.*

The six most northerly of the twenty roads originally under cover were totally demolished during the period 1951 to 1953, to create an open yard with five stabling and storage roads; the sixth road was cut short to the alignment of the front of the shed. GER locomotives had been sent all over the former LNER system since shortly after Grouping so it was no surprise to see a couple of the Stratford built 0-6-0Ts at Trafford Park both before and after Nationalisation. J67/2 No.68540 and J67/1 No.68595 snuggle up to N5 No.69304 beneath the remains of the soon to be demolished north section of the shed in 1951. BR sent the latter of these little GER 0-6-0Ts to the North-West in October 1949 for no other reason than to get some more service out of it because redundancy in its native patch was threatening soon after Nationalisation. No.68540 meanwhile had been at Trafford Park on and off since 8th October 1929 with a couple of short stints at Brunswick thrown in during the 1930s. No.68540 eventually left Trafford Park in February 1953 for Lincoln and in December 1955 it returned to its birthplace at Stratford where it was condemned and then cut up the following month – aged 63 years. No.68595 however was not so lucky in that respect. Transferring to Wrexham in December 1954, the six-coupled tank was condemned on the 8th January 1957, aged 57 years! It was hauled to Gorton for scrapping in February but from there it was then sent on to Doncaster for the last rites. *K.H.Cockerill.*

The variety continues! Former LNWR 'Cauliflower' 0-6-0 No.58427 resides in store at Trafford Park on 18th September 1955. This engine was allocated to Widnes at the time but with space for storing locomotives somewhat restricted at the Merseyside shed it was dumped at Trafford Park instead. The 2F was withdrawn by Christmas. *C.J.B.Sanderson.*

Captured on film 26th November 1964; two of Trafford Park's final classes of steam locomotive which ruled the roost during the final six years of the shed's life. From new, Fairburn Cl.4 tank No.42076 *(above)* worked on the Southern, latterly at Dover, until the end of 1959 when it was transferred to the LMR in exchange for BR Standard Cl.4 tanks. At first this engine was sent to Willesden where the change of scene and regime was a gradual progression from bad to worse. Shoeburyness and then Bangor were its next ports-of-call before ending up at 9E in January 1964. It was withdrawn in March 1967. Our other subject *(below)* was Stanier 8F No.48344 which came to 9E in May 1959 and is stabled outside a less crowded shed five years later. Along with the Stanier Cl.5s, the 8Fs did take the shed to closure. This engine moved on to Heaton Mersey in March 1968 but was withdrawn just days later. *both C.J.B.Sanderson.*

NEWTON HEATH

The north side of Newton Heath engine shed, at the western end, on Sunday 28th June 1959. This shows fifteen of the shed roads before work started on demolition of the southern side of the shed to make way for the diesel multiple unit shed. The roof style stems from the 1930s LMS design which was used to re-roof so many of the engine sheds inherited from the Lancashire & Yorkshire Railway, and other companies. On shed today is a typical mixture of ex-LMS standard passenger tanks, and tender engines plus a smattering of pre-Group types but the place wasn't bulging at the seams. On summer Sundays a large proportion of Newton Heath's passenger classes would be out working excursions to the Flyde coast or even the east coast, transporting those hardy souls who preferred the bracing cold of Scarborough or Bridlington to the balmy atmosphere of Blackpool, St Annes, or Southport. *C.Campbell.*

Until the final decade of steam, 'Royal Scots' at Newton Heath were something of a rarity. Occasionally a Polmadie 'Scot' might drop in after working one of the Glasgow (Central)–Manchester (Victoria) passenger trains but usually these expresses were in the hands of 'Jubilees' of which 26A had plenty. So the phrase about 'hen's teeth' comes to mind whenever 'Scots' and Newton Heath are mentioned in the same breath. However, all that was to change when, in April 1960, two of the class, courtesy of Longsight, and the re-routing of some of the Manchester (London Road)–London (Euston) expresses to Manchester's Exchange and Victoria stations whilst London Road was being transformed into Piccadilly! No.46106 GORDON HIGHLANDER and No.46137 THE PRINCE OF WALES'S VOLUNTEERS SOUTH LANCASHIRE were the chosen pair and during the year they contributed to getting Manchester's businessmen into London on the *MANCUNIAN* during its enforced diversion into Exchange. Those two returned to Western Lines sheds at the end of 1960 but in September 1961 Newton Heath was the recipient of four ex Kentish Town 'Scots': Nos.46133, 46139, 46140 and 46142 (it never rains but it pours!) which had been displaced by 'Peaks' on the Midland Lines. No.46139 was withdrawn in October 1962, No.46133 followed suit in February 1963 whilst the remaining pair moved to Longsight in June 1963. 26A's brief history of allocated 'Royal Scots' was over but a few visitors and indeed 'loaned' engines turned up later in the year. One such engine was Longsight's No.46129 which though no longer carrying its THE SCOTTISH HORSE nameplates, still had the backing plates attached and which remained with the engine all the way to the scrapyard. The 4-6-0 is depicted here at the west end of the shed on 3rd November 1963, ready for a day's work. *A.Ives.* 39

Alongside the unnamed 'Scot' was ex-Midland condenser–fitted 'Jinty' No.47207 receiving the attentions of its driver. Newton Heath had a long association with the Derby 3F 0-6-0T, mainly the LMS-built examples of which half a dozen were resident in 1935 (but only one at Nationalisation) and rubbing shoulders with the former Lancashire & Yorkshire 0-6-0ST which were in abundance at 26A. However, the ex-MR version of the 0-6-0T was something of a rarity on L&Y lines until Cricklewood and Kentish Town sheds started to cast off their large batches in the mid-1950s. Newton Heath got two initially, our subject here, and No.47212. Latter, in the 1960s, Nos.47202 and 47230 turned up, the latter for just a few weeks in 1963 but No.47202 came as late as August 1966 but was condemned by the end of the year after being one of the most photographed 0-6-0Ts of the decade. No.47207, when photographed in November 1963, was only a few months away from its demise which occurred in February 1964. *A.Ives.*

The east end of the shed on Sunday 3rd July 1966: With steam still operational in numbers, and vintage diesel shunters helping out the regular batch. The diesel fuelling pad presents an untidy and dirty mess whilst lubrication barrels are strewn about rather haphazardly. Another fuelling pad, mainly for multiple units, was located just to the right of the camera. This was the scene which greeted the visitor to Newton Heath – The British Locomotive Shed Directory stated: *'A broad path leads to the shed from the west side of Dean Lane, between Dean Lane and Newton Heath* stations. Walking time from either station less than five minutes'* – and during the decade of the 1960s spotters' watched as the original shed was slowly taken to pieces whilst the new sheds for the diesels were erected. When the original twenty–road running shed was intact, the Sunday morning visitor had to take a breath and decide where to start as upwards of 150 locomotives, nearly all in steam, simmered about the place. Even whilst you were plodding around the shed roads an engine could quietly leave the western end of the shed yard without your knowledge, and if it was one you required it was something of a disappointment to be told by fellow enthusiasts what was what! 'Those in the know' always walked through the repair shop to the west end of the yard towards the coaler just in case one was trying to sneak off shed. Remember, engines from Yorkshire, Scotland, and the far north-west of England, besides those from various Lancashire depots, visited 26A for coal, water, and temporary lodging. It was a vibrant place which always had something new to offer. *It was not physically possible to walk from Newton Heath station south along Dean Lane, from circa 1934. *A.Ives.*

41

The four road repair shed at Newton Heath was left intact when the first seven stabling roads of the running shed were demolished to make way for the five road diesel servicing shed in 1960. By the time this illustration was recorded inside the repair shed on 3rd July 1966, the diesel shed alongside had been fully operational for some years. The first thing of note, excluding the Standard 5, was the light airy atmosphere inside this place which was courtesy of all those sheets of glass in the roof. The roof, including those lovely timbers, was in fact the original 1876 hipped roof which had survived the decaying sulphurous smoke damage inflicted on the roof timbers of the adjacent twenty–road running shed which was re-roofed by the LMS in the mid–1930s. This place was sacrosanct and the men working in here had a reasonable chance of seeing rather than feeling the repairs they were carrying out. When it went dark fluorescent lighting came into their own – admittedly not until early 60s' – and just when winter arrived overhead blown-air heaters could be activated. The place was modern in steam days and one of the reasons why extensions were built at each end whilst the middle bit was left unchanged! So, on this Sunday in 1966 what was the Caprotti Standard 5 doing inside this place? Not yet ten years old, and looking decidedly like a withdrawn member of the class, Patricroft's No.73136 was in Newton Heath for repair and although showing all the signs of neglect, it was still very much an operational locomotive and would remain so until March 1968, filth and all. *A.Ives.*

No nameplate, no proper number plate, and no shed plate! BR 'Britannia' No.70049, formerly named SOLWAY FIRTH was another occupant of Newton Heath's repair shop on 3rd July 1966. Based by now at Upperby, this Pacific had seen better days and was actually the last of the class to be named, an event which took place as late as May 1960, six years after entering traffic! Although looking quite dirty, No.70049 was otherwise sound with little corrosion or signs of leaks although the plating behind that right hand buffer looks as though it has had a bump. For whatever reason this 'Brit' was in the shop, it was obviously rectified because it went back into traffic and at the end of the year was transferred to Kingmoor to join the remaining members of the class for another twelve months working prior to withdrawal. *A.Ives.*

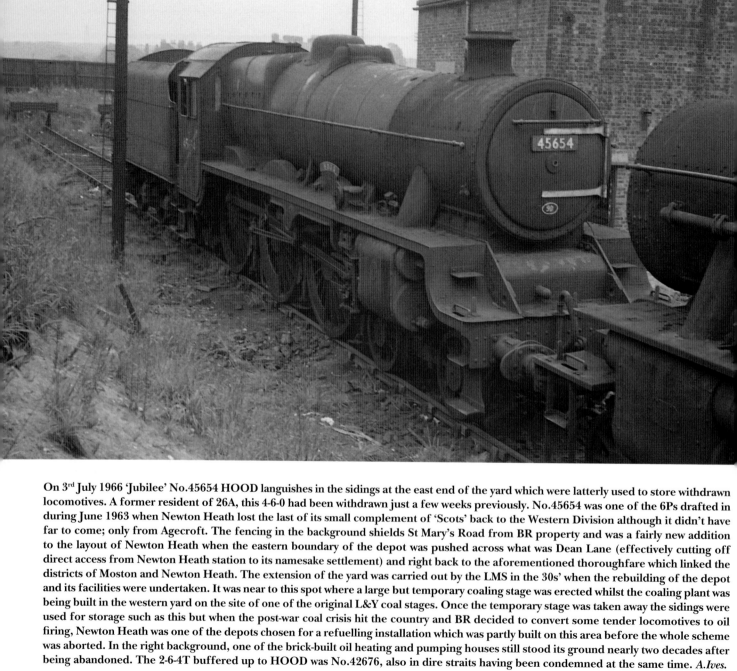

On 3rd July 1966 'Jubilee' No.45654 HOOD languishes in the sidings at the east end of the yard which were latterly used to store withdrawn locomotives. A former resident of 26A, this 4-6-0 had been withdrawn just a few weeks previously. No.45654 was one of the 6Ps drafted in during June 1963 when Newton Heath lost the last of its small complement of 'Scots' back to the Western Division although it didn't have far to come; only from Agecroft. The fencing in the background shields St Mary's Road from BR property and was a fairly new addition to the layout of Newton Heath when the eastern boundary of the depot was pushed across what was Dean Lane (effectively cutting off direct access from Newton Heath station to its namesake settlement) and right back to the aforementioned thoroughfare which linked the districts of Moston and Newton Heath. The extension of the yard was carried out by the LMS in the 30s' when the rebuilding of the depot and its facilities were undertaken. It was near to this spot where a large but temporary coaling stage was erected whilst the coaling plant was being built in the western yard on the site of one of the original L&Y coal stages. Once the temporary stage was taken away the sidings were used for storage such as this but when the post-war coal crisis hit the country and BR decided to convert some tender locomotives to oil firing, Newton Heath was one of the depots chosen for a refuelling installation which was partly built on this area before the whole scheme was aborted. In the right background, one of the brick-built oil heating and pumping houses still stood its ground nearly two decades after being abandoned. The 2-6-4T buffered up to HOOD was No.42676, also in dire straits having been condemned at the same time. *A.Ives.*

44

Class 4MT No.42656 shunts a lone Esso oil tank and attendant brake van in the east yard on Wednesday 22nd June 1966. The shed was situated to the left, as shown by the stabling roads fanning out, whilst a 70ft turntable, installed in 1936 was located further to the east up against the St Mary's Road fencing. In the right middle ground are the roads containing the withdrawn locomotives with the rear wall of Newton Heath station prominent. Between the station and the signal box can be seen the parapets of the bridge which carried the Rochdale line over Dean Lane. The 2-6-4T is just over the ground formerly occupied by the erstwhile lane before the LMS carried out the yard alterations in the 1930s; the lane ran in a straight line southwards from the bridge towards the left of the cameraman, roughly where the bunch of old sleepers are gathered. This view was captured from the top of the high wall built to block off Dean Lane at its southern end. Looking at this view from the summer of 1966, its seems amazing that another two years of steam locomotive operations were still ahead of this depot when the Eastern Region had basically banned steam south of Doncaster, the Western Region had totally eliminated steam, and the SR had managed to enclave their steam into the area which was once London & South Western territory. *K.Gregory.*

Setting off to work BR Standard Cl.4 No.80053 is awaiting its signal on 13th June 1953. This tank engine was one of five of the class (Nos.80049 to 80053) which came new to and then graced the roads at Newton Heath from the latter months of 1952 until September 1956 when they had been transferred away to Chester. Besides these five examples, 26A also took in Nos.80044 and 80046 during February 1956, with 80086 and 80093 arriving in the following June. They too were transferred away with the last one moving to Corkerhill in March 1960. Like their LMS counterparts, the useful BR Cl.4s worked much of the commuter traffic emanating from Manchester's Victoria station. The Cl.4 is at the shed outlet located at the western end of the yard in the fork of the Oldham branch and the ex-L&Y main line to Yorkshire. In the background is the former L&Y carriage and wagon works which was still carrying out repairs at this date. Out of sight to the left in this illustration was the other half of the rolling stock works, bisected from this group of buildings by Thorp Road thoroughfare. The carriage works was later renowned for producing concrete products for all manner of BR projects. *C.J.B.Sanderson.*

Everybody had the *Kitmaster* model of this 0-4-0ST didn't they? Not simply because it was cute and petite (shockingly small to a young lad just starting out with model railways and used to seeing 'Duchess of Atholl' and her ilk doing a scale 160 m.p.h. or so around the near 90 degree curves) but mainly because it was cheap, and easy to assemble with no complicated bits; which, on the face of it, was much like the prototype! No.51230 is stabled in a siding alongside the Oldham branch lines in the corner of the depot nearest Dean Lane station, on 13th June 1953. This is one of Agecroft's batch, sent to the parent shed for a bit of remedial work which couldn't be performed at 26B. The four-coupled tank was quite a stranger in the Manchester area and only Agecroft had a handful of them in BR days. Newton Heath's last foray with the class was during WW2 when three of them were allocated. However even then the diminutive engines could be found virtually nation-wide in places such as: Bath, Burton-on-Trent, Gloucester, Goole, Liverpool, Preston, Shrewsbury, and of course Agecroft – much the same as it was ten years previously. *C.J.B.Sanderson.*

One of the 'Breadvans' which were thrust upon Newton Heath and other local sheds during LMS days and which basically stayed well into BR days. These 2-6-2Ts had a lot of bad press (too much Derby influence in their design etc.) but their larger 2-6-4T sisters were superior not just in power output but mechanically too and were well liked by all who worked on them. But, back to the subject: No.40013 was photographed in the east yard on the afternoon of Saturday 13th June 1953 getting ready to stable for the weekend. Newton Heath got a couple of batches of these engines when they were new, starting with this example in 1930. In October 1945 they managed to get rid of it to Blackpool but after a year they sent it to Lostock Hall in 1946. Exactly a year later in October 1947 No.13, as it was then, turned-up back at Newton Heath like a bad penny! It then remained at 26A until withdrawn in December 1959. That though was not the end of the story because Nos.40014 and 40015 followed in the same tracks as 40013; Blackpool, Lostock Hall, 26A! The latter pair hung around longer too and were not condemned until May and March 1961 respectively. But there is more. Nos.40056 to 40061 and 40063, and 40065 all came new to Newton Heath, the final three clinging on at the Manchester shed until withdrawal. Nos.71 to 75 was a later batch which dispersed to other depots by the end of the decade. Nos.40056 to 40061 (56-61 then) were fobbed off to one of the garage sheds – nearby Lees – in April 1939 which put up with them until August 1954 when Botanic Gardens shed in Hull were the unwitting recipients of that lot! And so

48 the saga of Newton Heath's less than popular 'Breadvans' is told. *C.J.B.Sanderson.*

Waiting their turn to enter the repair shop, a pair of ex-L&Y 'A' Class 0-6-0s – only No.52334 being identifiable – and an ex-LMS Jinty, No.47586, fill three of the four roads outside the west end of the shop circa summer 1953. No.52334 was a relative newcomer to Newton Heath having been transferred from Bolton in February 1952 but its residence was to be fairly short because in December 1954 it was condemned. 3F No.47586 left 26A in 1954 for Rose Grove where it would spend the rest of its life until condemned in March 1960. *K.H.Cockerill.*

This is the life! The ubiquitous L&YR 'A' Class 0-6-0 could at one time be found all over the former LMS system in England and Wales but their stronghold was the old Central Division of the LMS and no place more so perhaps than Newton Heath. In 1935 for instance some twenty-six members of the class were allocated to 26A (Wigan Central actually housed twenty-eight) but in 1944 this number had risen to thirty-six! With Nationalisation that number had been halved six years later but the class were still represented in 1959 by a dozen of them such as No.52230 here which was on shed pilot duties on Saturday afternoon, 22nd August 1959. Newton Heath signal box and station form the background to this illustration captured in the east yard as the crew pose for the photographer. The 0-6-0 was a relative newcomer to 26A, and had arrived in June 1958 from Wigan Central after a six month sojourn there preceded by a transfer from Bangor the former LNWR shed which had used several 'A' class engines for decades. No.52230 was eventually withdrawn in April 1961, the class itself was diminishing quite rapidly at this time and although these useful engines had served their masters tirelessly since 1889, progress had to take precedence. Luckily one of their kind has been saved for posterity. *N.W.Skinner.*

Although Newton Heath's relationship with four-coupled steam locomotives basically petered out after Nationalisation, its friendship with 0-4-0 diesel locomotives got stronger after humble beginnings. This little gem is E.D.1 (Engineering Department No.1) which was part of the Departmental fleet and was looked after by the fitters at Newton Heath on behalf of the permanent way depot at Castleton near Rochdale. The 0-4-0 diesel-mechanical was built by John Fowler & Co. and was initially supplied to the LMS in 1935 – as their No.2 – to work the sleeper and creosote works at Beeston near Nottingham. At some point in its British Railways career the Fowler was sent from Beeston to Castleton and on 29th August 1959 it was stabled on Newton Heath shed. The ungainly looking locomotive was painted in an insipid green at the time and with its flowerpot style chimney was not the best advert for a diesel. When ED1 returned to its native heath is unknown but it was condemned in June 1962 and cut up at Derby works soon afterwards. In the background can be seen the carriage sidings known as Lightbowne Road yard and which are now also history, long gone beneath a residential housing estate. *N.W.Skinner.*

Another view of E.D.1 a month earlier, stuck in the same spot on road No.20 at the east end of the shed. Weighing in at exactly 25-tons, the 88 horsepower diesel had an engine with five cylinders! However, no slouch when it came to road work, it could run at up to 15 m.p.h. but the 30-gallon fuel tank must have restricted its movements somewhat. Newton Heath looked after further examples from Fowler's diesel-mechanical range in the shape of E.D.3 and E.D.6 which were both allocated to Castleton P.W. depot for a number of years. Slightly larger than ED1, these 1949 built diesels weighed four tons more and had 150 h.p. engines with four cylinders, larger wheels and fuel tanks but only a 10 m.p.h. top speed. They worked until September 1967. *A.R.Thompson.*

Further associations with four-coupled diesel locomotives occurred during the 1960s when Newton Heath received a new 170 h.p. Rolls-Royce engined, diesel-hydraulic – D2858 – from the Yorkshire Engine Company on Christmas Eve 1960. It remained the only one delivered new to the depot but more of the class were transferred in during 1963 as follows: D2869 13th July, ex Bank Hall; D2864 and D2865 3rd August, ex Warrington Dallam; D2866 2nd November, ex Agecroft; D2867 9th November, ex Bank Hall. This is D2867 outside east end of the extended repair shop on 26th November 1964. Just discernible is the legend 27A on the cast shed plate still fitted in the centre of the radiator cowling, a year after moving over from Liverpool. On 10th October 1964 D2859 was received from Derby. The filth clinging to the steam locomotives at this place was not confined solely to the old order, the newest members of the allocation at 26A were also able to indulge! *C.J.B.Sanderson.*

Somebody knows what the significance of the BP sign was adorning the front of Fowler Cl.4 tank No.42379 on the 26th November 1964 at Newton Heath. Withdrawn since the previous August, the parallel boiler 2-6-4T was the only one of its kind to be allocated to Newton Heath in BR times. Nine other members of the class, including four of the limousine cab examples, were resident at 26A from the mid to late 1930s until the spring and summer of 1946 when they dispersed to other sheds, mainly in Yorkshire. No.42379 arrived at Newton Heath in June 1963 and worked alongside its more modern sisters from the Stanier, Fairburn and Ivatt stables. This pair of 2-6-4Ts, the other is No.42280, were stored alongside the repair shop. In the left background, on the other side of the line to Oldham, stands the barracks. *C.J.B.Sanderson.*

Two Stanier products hold their own at Newton Heath on Thursday 26th November 1964. 8F No.48539 *(above)* stands on the east yard, whilst 'Jubilee' No.45578 UNITED PROVINCES *(below)* stables in the west yard. The 8F was just about to leave for its new home at Agecroft and its Newton Heath shedplate had been removed before the engine's release. No.45578 on the other hand had been withdrawn during the previous May but here it is in late November as large as life and, complete with nameplates! The date of the image is correct and verified. So, some mystery surrounds this locomotive's resurrection or otherwise. Does anyone know? *both C.J.B.Sanderson.*

This image of withdrawn Cl.3 0-6-0T No.47300 also affords a view across the east yard at Newton Heath on that November Thursday in late 1964 after recent changes had taken place around the depot. Coming in from the right is a section of the sweeping roof of the old engine shed with its 1935 style roof. Next in line is the new five road diesel depot with its central pitched roof and chevron painted doors, note the d.m.u. alongside the duel tanks. Just visible behind the boiler house chimney is the old repair shop, with its recently completed extension, and now looking for all the world as though it too is new. The depot's new admin block, with its glass and brick design is pure 1960s and is in stark contrast to the reminder of the past still visible on the skyline; the tall barracks block, which had enough beds to house 66 enginemen at any one time, was still doing business but not for much longer as traffic patterns changed. So, what of the derelict 3F tank? Having spent most of its working life in East London and spending much of the 1950s working its way north, No.47300 was one of the Hunslet-built members of the class (all except the final fifteen were supplied by contractors) and was put into traffic in 1924. A relative newcomer to the north-west of England, it had done little work since arrival and had lain here since withdrawal in August 1963. Looking at its position on the storage roads, it appears as though it is now being got ready to leave the depot for a scrapyard. The front window glasses have long disappeared, courtesy of the local children who often frequented this area of the depot, but otherwise it was very much intact, including the front numberplate – whatever happened to that? The exact date when No.47300 left 26A for the last time is unknown, likewise which yard eventually took it in (the depot code had changed to 9D shortly after the 0-6-0T had begun its slumber towards oblivion in September 1963, but it was not to know). *C.J.B.Sanderson.*

Looking as though it is stabled awaiting its next call to duty, WD 2-8-0 No.90708 was also recorded on the withdrawal lines at Newton Heath in November 1964. The tender had just been topped-up on Saturday 2nd May 1964 when something was found to be amiss during a routine inspection. Without further ado, the 'Austerity' was condemned and taken from the running roads to be unceremoniously dumped here alongside Newton Heath station. This engine had spent much of its BR life at Newton Heath – into traffic 3rd December 1949 – except for a period at Lees shed near Oldham, 7th June 1958 to 18th April 1964, from where it acquired the miniature snowplough and the hinged cabside windows. The 9D shed plate is still affixed and even the spectacle plates are intact, for the time being. Okay, who is going to empty that tender bunker? The tender of sister No.90371, another hapless WD which was withdrawn a week before our subject, projects into the left of the picture. *C.J.B.Sanderson.*

Another tender to empty! Stuck at the St Mary's Road end of the 'scrap line' on that Thursday in November 1964, was this 4F 0-6-0, No.44543, which had also been discarded as surplus. This Crewe built version of the Derby 4F was put into traffic in 1928 so was already thirty-six years old when condemned. The Fowler tender is one of those which were useful when travelling tender first in foul weather but became normal equipment for those engines pushing and pulling the large snow ploughs during and after blizzard conditions. The locomotive immediately behind the 0-6-0 is another Derby design, 3F No.47582, which was also 'up the creek without ...' Newton Heath station footbridge and some of the platform fencing is visible on the left but not for much longer because the station was closed on 3rd January 1966. Now then, let's look at another 'scrap line' developing at Newton Heath in November 1964. *C.J.B.Sanderson.*

Another area of 9D where withdrawn locomotives were stored 'Awaiting orders!' were a couple of sidings on the south side of the depot, alongside the Oldham branch. On 26th November 1964 WD 2-8-0s appeared to be the 'flavour of the month' for condemnation. 'Bog standard' WD No.90194 (*above*) had been brought down from Lees shed and condemned here on 21st March 1964. Spares had been cannibalised to keep other members going, especially bushes and the like from the motion. No.90548 (*below*) was a 9D resident and had been on and off for fourteen years since the 2-8-0 transferred from the Western Region in December 1950. Of course its WR origins were plain for all to see and one fixture, the fire-iron tunnel usually remained on ex-WR WDs which came to 'the other side' but the other piece of Swindonisation, the clack valves and their tall cover, were usually replaced for the more orthodox clack valves fitted to the majority of the class. So, it was unusual to find the Swindon clack cover nearly nine years after Swindon stopped maintaining this particular locomotive. *both C.J.B.Sanderson.*

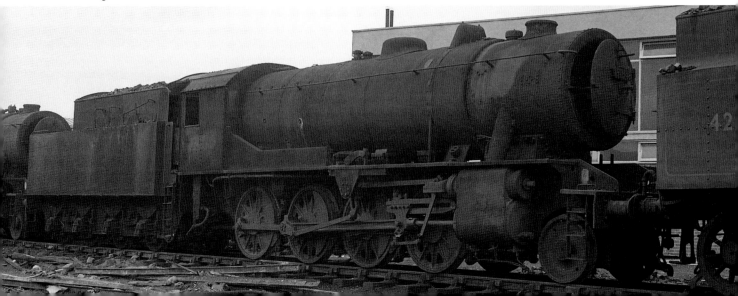

A regular visitor from Carlisle would come in the shape of one of their BR Cl.6 'Clans'. No.72009 CLAN STEWART was the appointed engine on Sunday 1st October 1961. Besides the Kingmoor engines awaiting the return working home, it was sometimes possible that Polmadie 'Clans' could also be found stabling at Newton Heath at the same time, but that event was more of a lottery than a sure thing to find such a combination (will anyone who has photographic evidence of such an event at 26A, with both engines in the frame, please contact the Publisher), Clan-Jubilee, Jubilee-Clan, Clan-Brit, Jub-Brit, not to mention the Stanier 5 combinations, were the norm. Note that our subject is not apparently carrying a name plate on this side of the engine! Something else worthy of note is the fact that the early BR emblem still adorns the tender some four years after the new crest was introduced. Nothing unusual about that you might think but since the crest was adopted in 1957, No.72009 had attended main works twice, one visit entailed a Heavy Intermediate repair where repaints were sometimes administered. However, this Clan kept the old emblem until September 1962 when Cowlairs gave No.72009 a Heavy General overhaul, a repaint, and the 'new' crest. Incidentally, this engine was the last of the class to receive a HG. *I.S.Jones.*

The ranks of the condemned grew in May 1967 and included seven Ivatt Cl.2s at Newton Heath; effectively bringing to an end to the link between the class and the depot. In recent years a further seven had ended their days at the shed. On Sunday 14th May 1967, No.46448 *(above)* looks despicably filthy in the east yard but it was only what we had come to expect by now. *(below)* No.46437 presents a different face though similar exterior on the same date. No.46490 separated them both. Note the 'fuel' mixture in the tender. *both A.Ives.*

GORTON

Gorton engine shed early on Saturday afternoon, 29th August 1959, with nearly all twenty (*see* later) of the running roads in view. On the right is the ten-road shed which lost a section of its roof and which was never restored. The shed on the left was rebuilt by British Railways and reduced to eight roads at the same time although that did not entail a re-arrangement of the trackwork (and pits!) but instead saw two of the stabling roads cut and their original shed access bricked-up. Both of the sheds date from 1879 when a massive increase in motive power saw the Manchester, Sheffield & Lincolnshire Railway invest huge sums of money in their Manchester locomotive base. A double-sided ramped coaling stage was erected in the area just behind where the photographer was standing and that facility served the shed for more than forty years until the LNER too saw fit to invest large sums in new mechanical plant. A selection of motive power on view includes the normal complement of 2-8-0s – O1, O4, WD – 0-6-0s – J11, J39 and ex-LMS 3Fs – 2-6-4Ts in the shape of a dozen Thompson L1s which were complemented, and soon to be replaced, by former LMR 2-6-4Ts – and K3s were also on shed. In 1948 some forty 2-8-0s were allocated along with a similar number of 0-6-0s. Assorted tank engines numbered another forty or so engines whilst approximately thirty 4-6-0s, comprising mainly Thompson B1s, formed the backbone of the express passenger fleet. A decade later the allocation had

declined in numbers but the variety of classes had nearly doubled; the closure of nearby Belle Vue shed in 1956 had sent a handful of former Midland types across the main line to Gorton even though it was still in the ER at the time. Noticeable by its gleaning front, the WD on the right, No.90369, was ex-works after a Heavy Intermediate overhaul and was now going through the running-in routine prior to being signed off by the works and returning to its home shed at Birkenhead. At Nationalisation Gorton shed came under Eastern Region control and its shed code was accordingly within the ER group being 39A; its so-called subordinate 'garage shed' 39B – to use the old LMS system of shed hierarchy and control, just as BR had done – was some thirty-odd miles away at Darnall in Sheffield. In February 1958, when massive regional boundary changes took place, Gorton became part of the London Midland Region and was re-coded 9H under the charge of Longsight. Two months later the code changed again to 9G when the former 9G – Northwich – was transferred into the Liverpool Edge Hill group and became 8E. The 9G code stuck with Gorton until closure, an event that took place on 14th June 1965. At closure, with some forty or so engines still on the books, not one of them was of GC or LNER origin. *N.W.Skinner.*

A view across the shed yard a few months earlier, on 28th June 1959, with former GCR types still prominent. J11 Nos.64298 and 64357, along with a couple of O4s fly the flag for the old order. Under the initial proposals for the Eastern Region shed codes drawn up in late 1948, Gorton was provisionally coded 45A with subs at Dinting, Hayfield and Macclesfield. Its garage sheds were to be Darnall 45B, Wrexham 45C and Bidston 45D – a large geographical area if nothing else. *C.Campbell.*

Five years on from the previous illustration and it was 'ABC' at the shed with the London Midland types, along with WD 2-8-0s, dominating the largely forgotten Cs, Js, Ns, and Os of the LNER! The date is 12th September 1964 and one hundred and twenty-seven years of locomotive servicing at Gorton is rapidly drawing to a close. The end came during the following summer when, on 14th June 1965, Gorton motive power depot ceased to exist as an operational entity. In the finality, its remaining locomotives were put into store to await buyers from the scrap merchants who would come, inspect and purchase. When the last of the rusty cold hulks were hauled away, the demolition gangs moved in. The first buildings to be demolished were those which were part of the locomotive works which had closed two years previously, well ahead of the engine sheds. Gorton was to be transformed from an industrial powerhouse to a modern wholesale fruit and vegetable market serving the greater Manchester area. Class 4MT No.42155 transferred from Edge Hill to Gorton in January 1963 but in September of that year it reallocated to Trafford Park working passenger traffic which regularly brought it to Gorton shed via changeovers at Guide Bridge. In November 1964 a final move took the 2-6-4T to Bolton where it was withdrawn in May 1965. This early afternoon view of the shed yard reveals the partly roofless shed where some years beforehand about a third of the roof was stripped. BR never did get round to rebuilding the place. *A.Vitty.*

The sunken ashpits at Gorton shed were in fact some distance from the main shed and were located alongside the main line at a place known as Priory Junction. The mechanical coaling plant was even further away, about a 100 yards west of this spot. The date is 28th September 1956, a Friday, and a sense of the LNER still prevails as C14 No.67443 holds centre stage and is supported by a J11 and an O4, both equally filthy. The Manchester, Sheffield, Wath catenary is now well embedded but steam locomotion still thrives in the area. The twin pitched roofs of the Belle Vue coaling stage can be seen in the middle background. *D.Fairley.*

Another fairly recent acquisition by Gorton in November 1963 was this Fowler 2-6-4T, No.42334. One of the most reliable and robust of the early LMS designs, these tank engines could be found all over the old LMS system from South Wales to Scotland, and on every division. In BR days they worked basically the same territory as they did pre-war but then started to appear at former LNER sheds especially on the former Cheshire Lines network where, from June 1957, they ousted not only the ex-Great Central tank engines but also the 4-4-0 passenger types. Gorton received the first representatives of the class in May of that year when Nos.42328 and 42374 arrived. They were followed in turn by 42326 and 42373 in November 1959. No.42361 came in November 1962 followed by 42334 and 42338 in June 1963; 42309 arrived in October 1963. 1964 saw No.42368 in January, 42327 in March, and finally 42369 in September. Most of the Fowler tanks mentioned above moved on when Gorton closed but a few were withdrawn at the shed. Our subject here came from the Midland shed at Leicester but transferred to Trafford Park in June 1965 only to be withdrawn during the week ending Saturday 25th December 1965 – the penultimate member of the class, and the oldest. None were preserved, a shame indeed when one looks at so much duplication of mediocre motive power within the preservation movement! *A.Ives.*

'Crabs', 'Black Fives' and various diesel shunters became the norm during those final couple of years prior to closure. Besides a thick coating of grime this so-called Horwich Mogul still sports a 9G shed plate in this Saturday 12th September 1964 illustration which is fitting because Gorton had been home for No.42760 since November 1959, and remained so until officially withdrawn on Wednesday 12th August 1964 which was just over a month prior to this scene being recorded. Why the 2-6-0 was still in traffic is unknown and when it was actually laid off is another unknown but the date of the photograph is correct. One theory suggests it may well be the motive power for a one-way train of condemned locomotives en route to a scrapyard but No.42760 was apparently cut up at Swindon. Any suggestions would be gratefully acknowledged. A.Vitty.

Much has been written about the LNER Garratt; most of the press being rather negative, especially in its latter lifetime when BR couldn't find a job for it. *(above)* Here in 1956 No.69999 resides on one of the shed roads at Gorton looking rather neglected but nevertheless reminding all who cast eyes on her what a big engine she was. *DRD Collection. (below)* This 18th June 1955 view showing the eight-coupled locomotive where it apparently spent much of its BR life, was taken in the works yard on yet another sunny day in Manchester. The works erecting shop form the backdrop. *F.W.Hampson.*

A long way from home, Tyne Dock allocated Thompson O1 No.63874 rests on the shed yard at Gorton on 1st October 1961. By some quirk of fate, this 2-8-0 had always been associated with former North Eastern sheds since it was put into traffic by the LNER as No.6630 after being purchased from the Government. At first, from 10th March 1928, it was allocated to Dairycoates in Hull but then transferred to the former H&B shed at Springhead. Its 'big move' came about in July 1940 when Heaton shed became its home until March 1944 when it was called into Gorton for rebuilding from O4/3 to O1. Re-entering traffic on 10th June 1944, No.6630 returned to Heaton but over the next seven years it undertook eight transfers – all within the North eastern area – until it finally settled at Tyne Dock shed on 2nd September 1951. The O1 had become No.63874 in February 1949 during a visit to the works at Gorton for a boiler change; both Darlington and Gateshead works had administered Casual Light repairs during BR days but all the major overhauls were undertaken at Gorton, the spiritual home of the O4s and Thompson O1 classes. The Westinghouse air pumps adorning the firebox side of 63874 were fitted at Gorton during the late summer of 1952 so that the 2-8-0 could take part in hauling the Tyne Dock–Consett iron ore trains in conjunction with the Raven Q7 0-8-0s which had similarly been fitted with the Westinghouse equipment. Four other O1s were also equipped for the workings. Note that a vacuum ejector was also fitted for controlling the braking of the iron ore trains; the two air pumps worked quite independently, one holding the wagon doors firmly closed, whilst the other opened them whilst the train was on the move over the discharge bunkers at Consett! So, why was our subject here at Gorton on the first day of October 1961? The reason is that the O1 was working from Gorton shed on a running-in schedule after a Casual Heavy overhaul (9th May to 2nd August 1961). On 12th August it re-entered works for rectification, not emerging until 2nd September. After this photographic record was captured, No.63874 went back to works on the last day of October for a month long Non-Classified repair. By mid-December it was back on Tyneside and managed another year of working before being condemned. It came back to Gorton and was cut up in January 1963. *I.S.Jones.*

The yard outside the chair and plate moulding shop, located at the eastern end of the works, was another venue for breaking up locomotives; such was the fate which awaited J11 No.64308 as a group of visitors roam around the works on a bright Sunday morning (it doesn't always rain in Manchester), 1st October 1961. After arrival at Gorton on 2nd September 1961 for an anticipated general repair and boiler change, the 0-6-0 was condemned some six days later. Luckily for us one of those Sunday visitors captured this scene on film; probably the final record of the J11's existence. Note the assorted 'bits' of locomotives and tenders ready to feed the iron foundry furnaces behind the tender of 64308, and also the frontal remains of another unfortunate victim lying on the ground beside the six-coupled engine; by the finish of work on Saturday 14th October, No.64308 was also lying on the ground in numerous pieces! Prominent in the left background is the original MS&LR roundhouse which, by this date, was in use as an iron foundry having been abandoned by the Running Department in 1879, and then given over to the locomotive works the following year. The former engine shed dated from 1848 – preceding the Locomotive Works by one year – and was unique in having a double track turntable, necessary to clear the huge central column which supported the massive roof. Nowadays that particular building would have been Listed and preserved but during the 1960s when BR were eager to sell the site of the works and engine sheds, it was demolished with indecent haste. Whilst we are in this area of the works, it is worth noting that the exact spot on which the J11 is standing was once the site of a three-road engine shed opened by the Midland Railway on 1st October 1866 (a Monday) which they vacated four years later with the opening of their roundhouse at Belle Vue. The MS&L took over the place thereafter and it too was utilised as a running shed until 1879 when it was vacated with the opening of the combined twenty-road sheds on Wellington Street. *I.S.Jones.*

Withdrawn D9 No.62302 resides temporarily on the siding alongside the boiler mounting shop on 29th April 1950. The main line on the left is bridged in the distance by the public footbridge known locally as 'The Birdcage' and which also spanned the works between the eastern end of the erecting shop and one of the machine shops. The substantial stationary boiler behind the row of discarded tenders supplied steam heating for the works. Anyone who knew this area of the works during BR days would remember the dozens of smokebox doors dumped on the ground just beneath the footbridge, the memorable part being that all of the doors still had number plates affixed! Back on the footbridge, the section in view led on the right to another steep flight of steps which elevated the bridge over the workshops below. The northern end of the footbridge consisted a long slope which became a racetrack for those on bicycles – one way at least. What of the 4-4-0? No.62302 had been condemned five weeks beforehand and was slowly making its way around the works until it got here. The next stop would be the yard outside the iron foundry; just a shunt away from this location. Latterly allocated to Brunswick shed in Liverpool, the D9 had spent nearly ten years working around the Midland & Great Northern lines of East Anglia during LNER days. Not quite fifty years old at withdrawal, No.62302 had nevertheless given good service to three different masters but now it is simply a memory just like most of the surroundings in this illustration. *K.H.Cockerill.*